KIRTAN

{CHANTING THE NAMES}

MANDALA
PUBLISHING
Your Publisher for Life
354 Bel Marin Keys Blvd., Suite D
Novato, CA 94949
t. 415.883.4055 • *f.* 415.884.0500
orders 800.688.2218
www.mandala.org
info@mandala.org

ISBN: 1-886069-78-6

Designed and printed by
PALACE PRESS
INTERNATIONAL
Printed in China

KIRTAN

{CHANTING THE NAMES}

TEXT BY

SWAMI B. B. BODHAYAN

MANDALA

PUBLISHING

Contents

THE LIFE OF CHAITANYA MAHAPRABHU

On March 7, 1486, the land of Bengal was blessed with the appearance of a great luminary. Sri Chaitanya Mahaprabhu, prophesized as the incarnation of divine love by the Vedic scriptures, was born in a Brahmin family in the town of Nabadwip, West Bengal, India.

Throughout his life, acquaintances affectionately referred to him by many names, such as Sachinandan, the son of Sachi, his mother. Because his birth took place under a neem tree, he was also lovingly called Nimai, especially during his childhood and youth. The townspeople knew him as Gauranga, because of his light, golden skin and physical beauty. Later in life, upon taking vows of renunciation, he would formally be given the name Chaitanya, and after his reputation as a great saint spread, the honorific title Mahaprabhu (great master) was further bestowed upon him.

Chaitanya's forefathers came from Sylhet in East Bengal, but had left their ancestral home to come to Nabadwip, which was then a great center of learning. They established the new family home on the banks of the Ganges, where Chaitanya's father Jagannath Mishra had been born. Chaitanya's mother Sachi was the eldest daughter of another Nabadwip scholar, the astrologer Nilambar Chakravarti. The young couple had eight successive daughters, but none survived childbirth. Finally, Sachi's ninth child, a boy named Vishwarupa, was born. Twelve years later, Chaitanya followed.

Chaitanya's birth corresponded with Krishna's spring swing festival, Dol Yatra, which is celebrated on the full moon day between February and March. Vaishnava theologians say that Krishna, who is always absorbed in the love of his precious gopis, accepted the mood and golden hue of the goddess Radharani and left his beloved Vrindavan to appear in his secret abode of Nabadwip, the hidden Vrindavan. In this incarnation, he flooded the land of Bengal with divine love and brought order back into the land's political, judicial and social orders.

Ordinarily, on the full-moon day, the moon proudly rises to bathe the world in pure, gentle rays of silver. On the Dol Purnima of 1486, however, there was an eclipse, as though nature was announcing that another moon, unique and divine, was also rising on that night—one that was greater in fullness, purity, coolness, gentleness, generosity, and poetic beauty than any ordinary moon, or indeed any other joy-giving thing in the world. As it was spring, the still leafless trees were filled with fresh new twigs and copper-colored sprouts. The mango buds were attracting swarms of buzzing bees in search of nectar, while the flower shrubs and creepers waved their branches and spread their fragrance in the wind. It was as though the goddess of nature herself was a young bride who, on hearing the jingling ankle bells of her groom, the Lord of the infinite worlds, had dressed herself in all her finery and was now eagerly awaiting his arrival for the wedding. Seeing nature take on such a beautiful aspect, one could easily conclude that this truly was the day that the Creator and His creation were to be united.

The ladies of the town blew their conch shells, filling the earth and sky with an auspicious reverberation. In every direction, the earth was filled with peace; the river waters were calm and even the ordinary plants and creatures seemed to be filled with joy. The world was awash with bliss. The sound of the Supreme Lord's name was on everyone's lips and all hearts overflowed with happiness. It was as though all were holding their breath in expectation of his appearance as Nimai, the son of Sachi.

At the very moment the world was filled with the sound of people everywhere calling out the names of God [in response to the eclipse], Krishna descended to the earth in his golden form.

(*Chaitanya Charitamrita* 1.13.94)

kali-kāle nāma-rūpe kṛṣṇa-avatāra
nāma haite haya sarva-jagat-nistāra

Krishna appears in this age of Kali in the form of his name. This entire universe will be saved by chanting the names of God.

(*Chaitanya Charitamrita* 1.17.22)

There is no religious practice in this age of Kali other than the chanting of the Holy Names. The Holy Name is the essence of all mantras—this is the fundamental meaning of all the scriptures.

(*Chaitanya Charitamrita* 1.3.99)

After Chaitanya's birth, astrologers assessed his birth chart in preparation for his name-giving ceremony. They concluded that, in accordance with the scriptures, the name Vishwambhar was appropriate, for it means one who supports, nourishes and protects (*bhara*) the universe (*viśvam*). Nevertheless, everyone continued to affectionately call him Nimai.

WHILE NIMAI WAS STILL very young, his brother Vishwarupa left home and became a wandering monk, never to return. As a result, when Nimai was of an age to begin his education, his parents resisted sending him to school, for they were afraid that if he became too educated, he would also become indifferent to worldly life and end up leaving home like his brother. In response to this, Nimai used his precocious intelligence to force his parents to send him to school. One day, Sachi Mata scolded Nimai for some childish misdemeanor, and the boy went off in

NIMAI BECOMES A SCHOLAR

a huff to sit on a pile of refuse. When she started to chastise him for getting dirty, Nimai cleverly answered,

> You won't let me go to school. I am supposed to be a Brahmin, but if I am not educated, how will I be able to distinguish good

from bad? I am illiterate, so how can you expect me to tell the difference between a pure place and an impure one? It's all the same to me. (*Chaitanya Bhagavat* 1.7.269-270)

After hearing Nimai speak in this way, Jagannath Mishra decided it was pointless to hold him back and so enrolled him in the school of Ganga Das Pandit. In a very short time, Nimai had mastered Sanskrit grammar and much more. If he encountered any scholar on the street, the cocky young lad would challenge him with trick questions about grammar or logic. The town's pandits would be embarrassed by their inability to answer Nimai and so would immediately cross the street to avoid him, but in fact, Chaitanya was teaching the real purpose of learning through his actions:

paḍe kene loka kṛṣṇa-bhakti jānibāre
se yadi nahila tabe vidyāya ki kare

What is the purpose of learning? It's to know about devotion to Krishna. If one does not learn this, then what is the point of being educated? (*Chaitanya Bhagavat* 1.12.49)

Jagannath Mishra died before Nimai had finished his schooling. Nimai dutifully performed the customary funeral rites for his father and then returned to concentrating on his studies. Before long, his reputation as a brilliant student had spread far and wide and he was able to open a small school and take students of his own.

At about this time, Keshava Kashmiri, a famous scholar who made his living by travelling and engaging other scholars in debate, arrived in Nabadwip. Nabadwip's pandits were afraid of being defeated by the Kashmiri Brahmin and losing their own reputations and that of the town itself as a center of learning. They consulted among themselves and decided to appoint Nimai as their representative. Their reasoning was that if the young scholar lost, no real harm would be done to Nabadwip's reputation; on the other hand, if he won, it would be a feather in everyone's cap. Were Keshava Kashmiri to be defeated by a mere boy, he would depart in shame and not bother to challenge any of the town's other scholars.

As soon as the two scholars sat down to their intellectual joust, Keshava Kashmiri composed a hundred extemporaneous verses in glorification of the Ganges. Nimai responded by focusing on only one of these verses and pointing out a number of errors in grammar, meter, vocabulary, and rhetoric. This made all the Kashmiri pandit's erudition seem tarnished, and everyone present applauded Nimai's brilliant victory.

Not long afterward, Nimai was married to Lakshmi Devi, the daughter of Vallabha Acharya. A few months after the wedding, he set off for East Bengal, or what is now Bangladesh, on a teaching tour to earn some money. His reputation was greatly enhanced on this trip, but when he returned, he found that Lakshmi Devi had been bitten by a snake during his absence and was no longer in this world. Seeing how grief-stricken his mother was, Nimai spoke the following words to console her:

> O Mother! Why are you so sad? How can anyone fight their destiny? In the passage of time, no person belongs to anyone else. That is why the Vedas always emphasize that this world is temporary. The whole creation is governed by the will of God. Who else but He brings us together or separates us from each other? If everything happens according to the will of God, then nothing should cause us distress! Furthermore, it is considered a sign of good fortune for a woman to die before her husband rather than being left a widow herself. Is Lakshmi not most fortunate? (*Chaitanya Bhagavat* 1.14.183-187)

For the next year, Nimai taught at the house of Mukunda Sanjaya. He would tutor his students from early morning until noon, and then pursue his own studies through the afternoon until late at night.

In the meantime, Sachi Devi became anxious to see her son married again. She engaged Kashinath Pandit to broker Nimai's marriage to Vishnupriya, the saintly daughter of Sanatan Mishra. Sanatan Mishra was a Brahmin from a respected family, a great devotee of Vishnu who possessed many good qualities: he was charitable, a welcoming host, truthful, and self-controlled. Furthermore, as a scholar to the royal court, he was very wealthy.

Another wealthy citizen of the town, Buddhimanta Khan, volunteered to finance the wedding. When the auspicious moment came, Nimai set off with great pomp in a festive wedding procession to Sanatan Mishra's house. The rituals were carried out, and the couple was united in marriage.

DESPITE BEING WED to a beautiful and virtuous wife, Chaitanya's interest in married life slowly waned. In early 1509, when he was nearly twenty-three years old, he traveled to Gaya in order to offer oblations at the holy Brahma Kund for the repose of his departed father's soul. After he had bathed in Brahma Kund and finished these sacred rites, Mahaprabhu went to Chakrabera Tirtha, where the famous temple to Lord Vishnu's lotus feet stands. While meditating there, Mahaprabhu heard someone reciting the glories of the Deity from the scriptures. He

CHAITANYA'S TRANSFORMATION

began to experience transcendental ecstatic symptoms; a veritable Ganges of tears flowed from his eyes.

While still in this condition, Mahaprabhu met Ishwar Puri, who was to become his spiritual master. As soon as they saw each other, they were both overwhelmed by waves of ecstatic love for Krishna. Mahaprabhu told Ishwar Puri that the actual purpose in coming to Gaya had been to meet him:

> My trip to Gaya became a success as soon as I saw your lotus feet. One who comes here to offer oblations delivers his forefathers and perhaps himself as well. As soon as I saw you, however, millions of forefathers were immediately delivered from their material bondage. No holy place could ever be your equal. Indeed, saints like you are the only real reason any holy place is able to sanctify the pilgrim. Please lift me out of this ocean of material entanglement. I hereby surrender my body and life to you. All I ask of you is that you please give me the nectar of Krishna's lotus feet to drink.
>
> (*Chaitanya Bhagavat* 1.17.50-55)

Chaitanya Mahaprabhu thus emphasized that the greatest benefit that comes from visiting places of pilgrimage is in meeting the holy people who frequent them. Therefore, no one should think that visiting a place of pilgrimage is ever equal to coming into contact with an authentic saint or spiritual master. The spiritual master is so powerful that he can bestow upon us a taste for the nectar of service to Krishna, the highest purpose in life according to Mahaprabhu.

The truth is that Chaitanya Mahaprabhu is the universal spiritual master; he is Krishna, incarnating as his own devotee in the mood of Radharani in order to distribute the means for attaining love of God. Nevertheless, in order to teach

the necessity of taking initiation from a bona fide spiritual master, he displayed this pastime of receiving the ten-syllable Krishna mantra from Ishwar Puri.

After initiation, Nimai became permanently intoxicated with devotion to Krishna. On his return home to Nabadwip, he was no longer the same proud but fun-loving scholar he had been. He was completely indifferent to all his previous preoccupations, including family life. He stopped teaching his students and even closed down his school. He spent all his time looking everywhere for Krishna, calling out Krishna's name and fainting due to separation from Krishna.

Soon thereafter, Nimai began to participate in kirtans, or ecstatic festivals of singing and dancing to the Holy Names of Krishna, in the house of Srivasa Pandit, an elderly Vaishnava who lived nearby. To this day, Srivasa's house is called the "Sankirtan Rasa Sthali," in comparison to the place where Krishna had his rasa dance with the gopis. Just as that was the most significant of Krishna's pastimes, sankirtan is the most significant of Mahaprabhu's pastimes. Mahaprabhu also held kirtans from time to time in the house of Chandrashekhar Acharya.

The vibrations of this kirtan washed over the land as far as Shantipur. Soon thereafter, all of Mahaprabhu's associates—Nityananda Prabhu, Advaita Prabhu, Hari Das Thakur, Gadadhar Pandit, Srivasa Pandit, Pundarik Vidyanidhi, Murari Gupta, Hiranya, Ganga Das, Vanamali, Vijaya, Nandanacharya, Jagadananda, Buddhimanta Khan, Narayan Pandit, Kashishwar, Vasudeva, Sriram Pandit, Sri Govinda, Govindananda, Gopinath, Jagadish, Sridhar Pandit and many others—came to join him in the nightly chanting.

This was the beginning of the sankirtan movement. It was as though the transcendental god of love had descended from the spiritual sky, conquering over the hearts of everyone and manifesting on their tongues in the form of Krishna's sweet name.

The atheists, to whom the body and this world are everything, could not understand what was happening to Mahaprabhu after his transformation, any more than a barren woman can understand what it means to bear a child. Those whose only obsession is their day-to-day existence and who have no comprehension of love for God are called pashandis. The pashandis of Nabadwip had differing opinions about Mahaprabhu's kirtans, but all were against it. Some said that the devotees were disturbing the peace with their meaningless noise making; others thought they were just drunkards partying. The pashandis criticized and condemned, each according to their own misunderstanding, but the devotees paid them no attention. They simply remained absorbed in singing the Holy Names with Nimai.

OBSTACLES TO THE SANKIRTAN MOVEMENT

When the pashandis saw they were unable to put a stop to the kirtan with their negative propaganda, they went to complain to the magistrate, or Kazi, who was the local representative of Bengal's Muslim ruler. The Kazi ordered the kirtan to be stopped, but Nimai refused to obey such an unjust dictate. He proclaimed, "No one has the authority to stop the chanting of the Holy Names in this age of Kali."

> He ordered the devotees, "Go and perform kirtan. Today I will put all the Muslims in their place! Light torches in every household. We'll see if the Kazi has the nerve to stop us!
>
> (*Chaitanya Charitamrita* 1.17.130,134)

> Today we will hold kirtan throughout Nabadwip. We'll see who dares stop us. If we have to, we will burn down the Kazi's house and see what the king does about it. Today I will send down a great shower of love for Krishna. The non-believers will meet their maker today!
>
> (*Chaitanya Bhagavat* 2.23.121-123)

Nimai marshalled all the Vaishnavas and their sympathizers into a huge protest march, and fearlessly led the procession of chanters through the town up to the Kazi's house. Once there, the agitated townspeople started to vandalize the house, flower gardens and orchards. The few soldiers the Kazi had were insignificant in number compared to the large numbers of townspeople who had taken Nimai's side.

The Kazi was frightened by Nimai's fearsome form and barricaded himself inside the house, keeping himself invisible. Nimai became angry when the Kazi refused to meet with him and said,

> Where is that little rascal Kazi? Bring him here right away or I'll have his head cut off! Surround the house and set fire to it. Let him and his family burn to death. I will destroy anyone who opposes the chanting of the Holy Names. (*Chaitanya Bhagavat* 2.23.388, 399, 402)

When the Kazi realized that he was surrounded by crowds of people carrying flaming torches closing in on him, he knew that there was no way out. In the meantime, some of the devotees were concerned to see how angry Mahaprabhu was and tried to calm him down. On hearing the devotees' appeal, Chaitanya composed himself, and his world-destroying Shiva spirit faded away.

Nimai and the other devotees sat down in front of the Kazi's front door. Nimai sent one of Nabadwip's most respected citizens inside to see the Kazi and announce his demands. When the Kazi was assured that Nimai meant him no harm, he was relieved and came outside. He courteously welcomed Nimai Pandit to his home and Nimai answered him with the respect appropriate to a member of the ruling class. They then established a certain intimacy when the Kazi called Nimai "nephew" and Nimai responded by calling him "uncle" (*māmā*). In Bengal, everyone has "village relations" beside their natural family relations. The Kazi came from the same village as Nimai's mother Sachi, and as such he was Sachi's "village" brother and Nimai's uncle, even though they belonged to mutually exclusive social classes.

In those days, not only would Brahmins refuse to speak with Muslims, but if they were even touched by a Muslim's shadow they were obliged to take a bath in the Ganges to be purified. It was thus very unusual for the high caste Nimai to engage in such a close exchange with the magistrate.

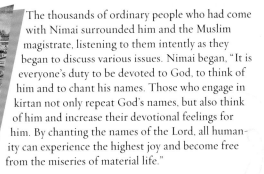

The thousands of ordinary people who had come with Nimai surrounded him and the Muslim magistrate, listening to them intently as they began to discuss various issues. Nimai began, "It is everyone's duty to be devoted to God, to think of him and to chant his names. Those who engage in kirtan not only repeat God's names, but also think of him and increase their devotional feelings for him. By chanting the names of the Lord, all humanity can experience the highest joy and become free from the miseries of material life."

Nimai's charming and humble manner, sweet voice and deeply reasonable discourse charmed the Kazi. He concluded,

hindūra īśvara baḍa yei nārāyaṇa
sei tumi hao hena laya mora mana

The Supreme Deity of the Hindus is Narayan. I get the impression that you are this Narayan.
(*Chaitanya Charitamrita* 1.17.215)

The people all watched and waited to hear what Nimai would say in answer to the Kazi's startling words of praise. Nimai punctured the charged atmosphere with a laugh.

> Mahaprabhu gave the Kazi a familiar touch, and began to answer, "You have spoken Krishna's name. This is truly wonderful. During our conversation you have uttered the names Krishna, Hari and Narayan. You are most fortunate and pious."
> (*Chaitanya Charitamrita* 1.17.216-218)

Of course, it was also unheard of for an ordinary citizen to touch a member of the ruling class in this familiar way. However, the Kazi was so caught up in the emotion of the situation he had forgotten all about the proper protocol. He simply gazed at Nimai's beautiful face, his eyes watering, and mentally surrendered himself to his lotus feet. He then prayed to him for the gift of love of God.

prabhura caraṇa chuṅi' bale priya-vāṇī
tomāra prasāde mora ghucila kumati
ei kṛpā kara yena tomāte rahu bhakti

He touched Mahaprabhu's lotus feet and spoke sweetly to him. "My wickedness has been dissipated by your blessings. Now be kind and bless me again that I may always have devotion to you."
(*Chaitanya Charitamrita* 1.17.219-220)

In this way, the prohibition against kirtan was lifted and all the orchestrations of the pashandis were thwarted.

The tomb of Chand Kazi still stands in the village of Baman Pukur not far from Nabadwip and people of both Hindu and Muslim faiths come there to offer their respects and salaams to his memory. Some historians say that this demonstration led by Nimai in defense of sankirtan was the beginning of the Indian freedom movement.

ONCE THE OBSTACLES presented by the kazi were removed, Nimai could freely perform kirtan wherever he wanted. As proof of the power of the Holy Names, many of those very atheists who had been inimical to the chanting were now converted. Significant among these converts were the two brothers Jagai and Madhai. So degraded was this pair that the only sins they had not committed were those that had not yet been invented. They spent all their time in the company of their drunken cronies, but even so, they had been spared the occasion to blaspheme devotees of the Lord. This

THE SALVATION OF JAGAI AND MADHAI

was their one saving grace.

Lord Krishna appeared as the son of Sachi in this present age of Kali to spread the chanting of the Holy Names. He thus ordered his beloved associates Nityananda Prabhu (affectionately known as Nitai) and Hari Das Thakur to go from door to door to ask people to chant the Holy

Names. One day, as they were going through the town carrying out this order, they happened upon Jagai and Madhai. It was as though destiny had brought them together so that Nitai, the savior of the most fallen, could shower his mercy upon them.

Nitai was sometimes called "Avadhut," which is a type of renunciate who is outside the social norms. As soon as Madhai heard the word "Avadhut" pronounced, he became senselessly angry and picked up a piece of a broken pot lying on the ground and hurled it at Nitai, cutting his forehead. Nitai's head started to bleed, but rather than becoming angry himself, he remembered Chaitanya's order and continued glorifying Krishna to the two sinful brothers.

In the meantime, Chaitanya, who is present in the soul of all creatures, had become aware of these events and rushed to the scene in the company of his other associates. On seeing Nitai's wound, he became so angry that he started calling for Sudarshan, his disc shaped weapon.

Madhai fell down at Nitai's feet and begged him repeatedly for forgiveness. Nitai is the personification of compassion and so harbored no resentment against Madhai; indeed, he forgave him immediately. The two brothers became so remorseful that they promised Nitai to henceforth stop all sinful activities and commit themselves to the chanting of the Holy Names and the service of

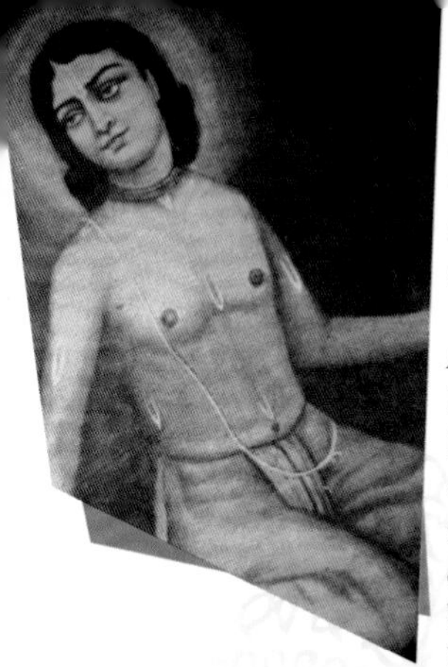

Mahaprabhu's devotees. Chaitanya and all his companions then softened their attitude toward the brothers and absolved them of their transgressions, even destroying their criminal tendencies.

After being blessed by Nityananda Prabhu, Jagai and Madhai began to burn with remorse for all the sins they had committed in their lives. They started to keep the company of devotees and commenced an intense regimen of prayer and meditation. They gave up all their evil companions and gradually forgot their past. In time, they both became great devotees. Mahaprabhu even warned his disciples that they should never think less of the two brothers because of their previous immoral activities. Now that they had been transformed, their lives as sinners were to be forgotten.

Nityananda ordered Madhai to constantly chant Krishna's name and to serve the Ganges River by cleaning the steps leading down to the ghat, or bathing place, and to ask everyone for forgiveness, prostrating himself in front of those who came there to bathe. Madhai would thus regularly come to the riverbank and remove the accumulated silt and waste with a shovel. Visitors to Nabadwip still visit this holy site, known as Madhai Ghat, today.

This pastime reveals many things about the spiritual path taught by Chaitanya Mahaprabhu. He himself was a Brahmin of the highest caste. Hari Das Thakur, on the other hand, was born in a Muslim family and Nityananda Prabhu, as an Avadhut, was outside the caste system. By asking Hari Das to become the teacher of the Holy Name, and by saving Jagai and Madhai through Nityananda Prabhu, Mahaprabhu taught that the teacher of spiritual truth is beyond human designations like caste, class or race. Through this pastime, he also taught that those who advocate the chanting of the Holy Names or the teachings of Krishna should never do so out of a desire for material profit. There is no greater offense than using God or religion as a business.

There is also a special secret hidden within Mahaprabhu's pastime of calling for his Sudarshan weapon. Narottam Das Thakur taught that even negative emotions such as anger can be used in the service of Krishna. He sang, "Use your anger against those who are inimical to Krishna *(krodha kṛṣṇa-dveṣi-jane)*." In other words, in certain cases, being angry is not against one's own spiritual welfare. We see this also in the example of Hanuman, the monkey chief of the Ramayana who served Lord Ramachandra by showing anger toward the demon Ravana.

DURING THE YEAR that Mahaprabhu inaugurated the sankirtan movement in Nabadwip, he performed many wonderful pastimes in the streets and homes of its residents. Through these pastimes, he revealed all six traits proclaimed by the Vedic literature to be characteristic of divinity: wealth, bravery, fame, beauty, knowledge and renunciation.

Then came another event that signaled the turning in Mahaprabhu's life. One day, he was sitting quietly at home, absorbed in the mood of a gopi, or cowherd girl, separated from

MAHAPRABHU TAKES SANNYAS

Krishna and angry with him for his lack of compassion in abandoning her. In this state, Mahaprabhu repeated over and over again the word, gopi, gopi. One of his students, a pashandi, happened to overhear him and challenged him, "Why are you chanting the names of some women instead of the names of Krishna?

What do you gain by repeating 'gopi, gopi'?"

Mahaprabhu thought the student was there to plead on behalf of Krishna, towards whom, absorbed in the mood of a gopi as he was, he was still feeling angry. He reacted angrily and started to accuse Krishna of unfaithfulness and all manner of flaws. The poor student was completely unable to comprehend Mahaprabhu's words, but protested at what sounded to him like blasphemy. Mahaprabhu then picked up a stick and started to pursue the boy who fled in fear of his life. When the student told the other Nabadwip Brahmins what had transpired, they plotted to have some thugs punish him for his transgression by beating him.

The inability of the town's Brahmin community to understand him and their reaction to this incident saddened Mahaprabhu, who spoke the following riddle in response to it:

karila pippali-khaṇḍa kapha nivārite
ulaṭiyā āro kapha bāḍila dehete

> I took a piece of pippal fruit as a medicine for my cough. But instead of curing my problem, it has simply made my cough worse.
> (*Chaitanya Bhagavat* 2.26.121)

In other words, "I have shown so many wonderful pastimes in order to teach these people about spiritual life, but they have not been able to understand anything. Indeed, they are becoming inimical to pure devotion." He concluded that he had to take extraordinary steps to remedy the problem and save them:

ataeva avaśya āmi sannyāsa kariba
sannyāsīra buddhye more praṇata haibe

> So I must take the renounced order of life. If I take sannyas, people will respect me simply because of my station in life.
>
> (*Chaitanya Bhagavat* 2.26.122)

In this way, Mahaprabhu decided to follow the social custom of taking sannyas. At around the same time, Keshava Bharati came through Nabadwip on his way to his ashram in Katwa, and Mahaprabhu revealed his intention to him. He only told five other people: his mother Sachi Devi, Gadadhar Pandit, Chandrashekhar, Mukunda and Brahmananda. However, the secret was badly kept and soon everyone in town knew about it, with the exception of one person—his wife, Vishnupriya Devi. Sanatan Mishra's daughter Vishnupriya had come to Mahaprabhu's house as his wife, bringing with her so many hopes and dreams for a lifetime of conjugal happiness. Even so, she had never been able to feel real peace of mind, as she had long watched her beloved husband become more and more absorbed in spiritual life. Her fears had thus grown that he would one day leave her and take sannyas.

On the day before Chaitanya planned to leave, he spent the entire day in kirtan with his companions. Then, at the end of the day, he bid farewell to them

all, knowing that he would soon be leaving them forever. He then returned home, where Sachi Mata and Vishnupriya were waiting. Vishnupriya brought water to wash his feet, as was the custom. Nimai went through the customary duties of a householder Brahmin—performing his evening meditation and worship, eating sanctified food and talking with his mother for a while before finally going to his room to rest.

There, the desolate Vishnupriya joined him. It seemed as though the clouds of imminent separation were gathering in the lonely room. Her anxious questions rumbled like thunder before a storm. The beautiful Vishnupriya herself was like a flash of lightning illuminating Nimai's body. And finally, tears began to pour from her eyes like the rains at the height of the monsoon season.

Vishnupriya's emotions also affected Nimai. Though he had made his decision to leave everything and commit his life completely to the pursuit of devotion to Krishna, he now felt his determination wavering. The moment was dramatic, and the emotions intense. He beckoned to her to come closer and held her in his arms, telling her of all the love he felt for her in his heart. Thus reassuring her, he was able to calm her spirit.

Then began the pastimes poets so love to describe, where a lover and his beloved prepare for union. Nimai dressed Vishnupriya in her finest sari and helped her put on her golden ornaments. The room glowed with the flame of a love that was devoid of the least touch of lust. When the night came to an end and Vishnupriya was fast asleep, Nimai cut through his attachments and affections and slipped out of the house. In a few hours he would arrive in Katwa, shave his head and become a sannyasi.

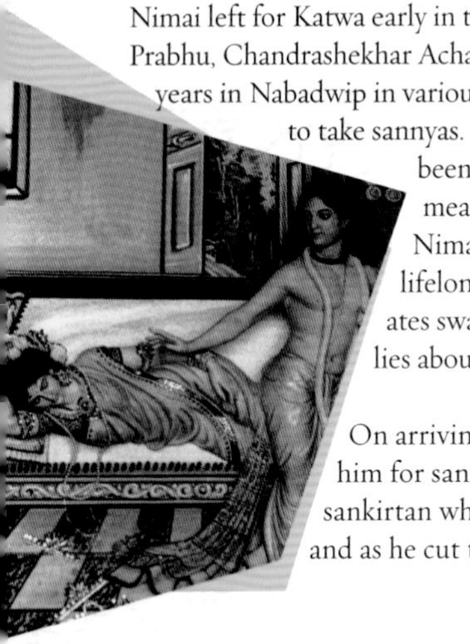

Nimai left for Katwa early in the morning with three companions—Nityananda Prabhu, Chandrashekhar Acharya and Mukunda Datta. He had spent twenty-four years in Nabadwip in various wonderful pastimes, and now he was setting off to take sannyas. They first went to the Ganges, in the place that has been immortalized as Nirdaya Ghat. The word *nirdayā* means "bereft of compassion," for by leaving Nabadwip, Nimai seemed to be acting most cruelly to all his family, lifelong friends and companions. He and his three associates swam across the river and then made for Katwa, which lies about ten miles to the north on the other bank.

On arriving at Keshava Bharati's ashram, Mahaprabhu begged him for sannyas. His companions stood by and performed sankirtan while he danced. A barber was called to shave his head, and as he cut through Mahaprabhu's beautiful tresses, he and all

the other devotees shed tears of distress.

As the day drew to a close, Mahaprabhu whispered a mantra he had received in a dream into Keshava Bharati's ear and asked him whether this was indeed the sannyas mantra. It was Mahaprabhu's wish that Keshava Bharati repeat this very same mantra to him, by speaking it into his ear according to the custom. In fact, by first repeating it to Keshava Bharati, Chaitanya Mahaprabhu was in effect blessing him by making him his disciple. Keshava Bharati gave Nimai the name Krishna Chaitanya. In his new saffron clothing, he looked extraordinarily beautiful.

Meanwhile, in Nabadwip the news quickly spread that Nimai had left to take sannyas. Sachi Devi had lost her son and herself in lamentation. Vishnupriya shed tears incessantly. She felt herself so alone—she was still so young, not yet a woman, and now she was watching the only possibility for future happiness shatter before her eyes. She seemed to have fallen into a shoreless expanse of water, where she was drifting without any direction.

Vishnupriya was to incarnate the mood of love in lifelong separation. The intensity of her emotions perhaps even exceeded that of Radharani, who suffered so much in a previous age after Krishna left for Mathura. After all, Radharani always had the hope that Krishna might one day come back, but Vishnupriya could not even hope for that much.

The other devotees were also affected by Mahaprabhu's departure. The town was filled with the sounds of their lament, the memory of which still washes over the world, communicating their suffering. The Lord's devotees still look up to the empty sky and sing the words immortalized by Govinda Ghosh:

hede re nadiyā vāsi kāra-o mukha cāo
bāhu pasāriyā gorā cāndere phirāo

> O citizens of Nadia! To whom will you now turn? Raise your arms to the heavens and pray for our golden moon to come home!

After being ordained a sannyasi, Mahaprabhu left Katwa and went to Shantipur. A messenger went to Nabadwip to tell Sachi, who came there to see him. Sachi asked him not to go to Vrindavan, as had been his original intention, but to go instead to Jagannath Puri, where she would be more likely to get news of him.

Mahaprabhu reached Puri in March of 1510. When he first arrived there, he went to see Lord Jagannath in the temple. The sight of the Deity sent Mahaprabhu into an ecstatic trance, falling to the ground in a faint. Sarvabhauma Bhattacharya, a great scholar of Vedanta, happened to be there at the time and, impressed by the young sannyasi, took him to his own home. The devotees who had accompanied Mahaprabhu revived him with their chanting of the Holy Names.

When he returned to consciousness, Sarvabhauma Bhattacharya proposed that Mahaprabhu take philosophy lessons from him: he would teach him everything he knew about the monist, or Mayavada, philosophy. Mahaprabhu agreed and for seven days the scholar explained the Vedanta Sutras according to Shankara's commentary while Mahaprabhu listened without saying a word. On the eighth day, however, Sarvabhauma became somewhat troubled by Mahaprabhu's silence and asked whether he had any questions. Mahaprabhu responded that though he found the aphorisms of Vyasa Deva very easy to understand, the explanations given by Shankara obscured their crystal-clear meaning. Shankara's commentary, he posited, went against the Vedanta. Lord Shiva appeared as Shankaracharya in the age of Kali to invent this non-dualist philosophy in order to bewilder the atheists. The true interpretation of the Vedanta is the philosophy of simultaneous oneness and difference. The Mayavadis are disguised atheists, he said.

veda nā māniyā bauddha haya ta nāstika
vedāśraye nāstikya-vāda bauddhake adhika

> The Buddhists are called atheists because they do not accept the Vedic authority. The Mayavadis, however, are worse than the Buddhists, because they preach atheism on the basis of the Vedic literature.
> (*Chaitanya Charitamrita* 2.6.168)

Mahaprabhu proved his point with reference to the scriptures and was able to convince Sarvabhauma Bhattacharya of his conclusions.

After this, Bhattacharya expressed a desire to hear Mahaprabhu explain a verse from Srimad Bhagavatam, *ātmārāmāś ca munayaḥ* (1.7.10). Mahaprabhu first asked Bhattacharya to explain his understanding of the verse. Sarvabhauma gave nine possible interpretations, employing his full intellectual prowess and scholarship. After he finished, Mahaprabhu began to give his own explanation. Without even touching on Sarvabhauma's version, he elaborated on its meaning in eighteen different ways, completely astonishing the scholar. Sarvabhauma then surrendered fully to Mahaprabhu, who showered his mercy on him by giving him visions of his various divine forms. Mahaprabhu also blessed him with a clear understanding of the divine truths.

ĀTMĀRĀMĀŚ CA MUNAYAḤ

A MONTH LATER, in April of 1510, Mahaprabhu left on pilgrimage to southern India. He wanted to go alone and told all his associates as much. Nityananda Prabhu insisted however, that he take a servant. As a result, Mahaprabhu agreed to allow Krishna Das, a Brahmin, to accompany him. Sarvabhauma gave Mahaprabhu a few pieces of cloth and asked him to stop near the Godavari River and meet with Ramananda Raya. Nityananda and the other devotees went with Mahaprabhu as far as Alalanath, where they said their goodbyes.

SOUTH INDIAN PILGRIMAGE

On the road, Mahaprabhu chanted the Holy Name in the mood of a gopi in separation from Krishna. He transformed anyone he encountered into Vaishnavas. It seemed as though Mahaprabhu was being even more merciful to the people of South India than he had been to his neighbors in Nabadwip, revealing his generosity and compassion to everyone he saw.

When Mahaprabhu arrived at a holy town called Kurmasthan, he visited the temple of Kurma Deva and offered the deity prayers and praises. He found lodgings with a local Brahmin and while there, another Brahmin named Vasudeva Vipra came to see him and begged for his mercy. Vasudeva was seriously ill with leprosy, his body covered with open sores. Mahaprabhu showed his kindness by embracing him and, in so doing, immediately cured him of both his physical and spiritual malaise. He then designated him an acharya, or spiritual teacher, and bestowed on him the name Vasudeva Amrita-prada, "Vasudeva, the giver of immortality."

Mahaprabhu continued on his way to the Godavari. Crossing the river, he came to Rajamundry and from there to Goshpada Tirtha. There he observed a man being carried in a palanquin, surrounded by numerous Brahmins and accompanied by a fanfare of bugles and drums. Recalling the descriptions Sarvabhauma had given him, Mahaprabhu recognized this person as Ramananda Raya. When Ramananda saw the effulgent sannyasi standing by the side of the path, he got

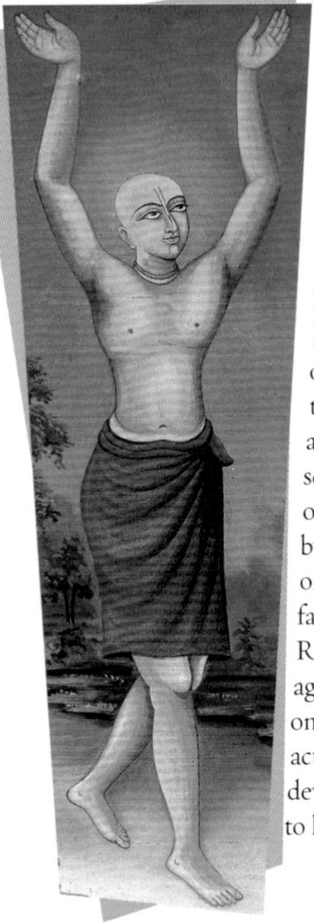

down from his elevated seat and prostrated himself on the ground. Mahaprabhu lifted him and embraced him tightly. Waves of divine love rolled over both of them. Ramananda asked Mahaprabhu to stay there for a week or so, so that they could talk about Krishna together.

Mahaprabhu found room and board in a Brahmin's house. Then, in the evening, Ramananda came to see him dressed in humble attire. He prostrated himself on the ground as a gesture of humility. Mahaprabhu then asked Ramananda to explain the purpose of life and the means for attaining it, with reference to the scriptures. Ramananda's first answer was that the goal of life is devotion to God, and because God is pleased by the execution of one's duties within the worldly social order, that was the means for attaining it. This answer failed to satisfy Mahaprabhu, who said it was superficial. Ramananda smiled and gave another answer, which again was judged superficial by Mahaprabhu. One by one, Ramananda suggested devotion mixed with fruitive activities, taking shelter of the Lord (sharanagati), and devotion mixed with the cultivation of knowledge—only to have each response rejected. Finally, when he arrived at devotion without any hint of the cultivation of knowledge, Mahaprabhu said, "This is correct, but surely you can go even further."

Ramananda said, "Better than exclusive devotion is devotion in ecstatic love." Mahaprabhu was satisfied with this response also, but nevertheless asked Ramananda to go even further. Pressed in this way, Ramananda went on to explain love for Krishna in the moods of servitude, friendship, guardianship, and finally that of romantic love. The mood of romantic love is present in the spiritual world, where the transcendental milkmaids of Vrindavan feel spontaneous love for Krishna. In our world, sexuality is an illusory source of happiness, because this world is a perverted reflection of the spiritual world. Thus everything here is the opposite of its corresponding transcendental image. As such, this mood in love for Krishna is elevated and desirable, while the so-called romantic love of this material world proves problematic and unsatisfying.

Mahaprabhu thus accepted love for Krishna in the mood of the gopis as the supreme and ultimate mood of devotion. Then Ramananda began to glorify Srimati Radharani, the best of all of Krishna's mistresses. According to the *Nārada-pañcarātra*, Radharani is the queen and presiding deity of the divine Rasa dance, where the loving exchange between Krishna and the gopis has its ultimate expression.

rāsādhiṣṭhātrī devī ca
svayaṁ rāseśvarī parā

vṛndāvane ca sā devī
paripūrṇatamā satī

Radha is the presiding deity of the Rasa dance. She is the queen of the Rasa dance. She is the supreme goddess in Vrindavan and the most perfect and complete of all chaste women.

The *Nārada-pañcarātra* also states:

yathā brahma-svarūpaś ca
śrī-kṛṣṇaḥ prakṛteḥ paraḥ
tathā brahma-svarūpā sā
nirliptā prakṛteḥ parā

Just as Krishna is the form of Brahman and beyond the material nature, so too is Srimati Radharani, who is untouched by matter.

In response to Mahaprabhu's questions, Ramananda began to describe the mood of love in separation, finally coming to the *prema-vilāsa-vivarta* at the very highest stage of Radharani's love for Krishna. As an example of this, he sang a song of his own composition, beginning with the verse:

pahilehi rāga nayana-bhaṅge bhela
anudina bāḍhala avadhi nā gela

> At first, my attraction to Krishna arose out of the way he looked at me. From then on, it simply increased, without ever reaching a limit.

After talking about this ultimate stage of divine love, Mahaprabhu asked Ramananda how it was possible for an ordinary human being to attain it. Ramananda answered that the only way such service could be had was to follow in the footsteps of the gopis. This is the highest possible attainment of human life.

Mahaprabhu was very pleased with his conversations with Ramananda. Later, Ramananda retired from his post as governor and, with the king's permission, came to live in Puri so that he could remain in Mahaprabhu's company.

Mahaprabhu continued his pilgrimage through southern India before returning to Puri where he was given lodging in the house of Kashi Mishra, the spiritual master of the king himself. Once situated there, Mahaprabhu ordered Nityananda Prabhu to return to Bengal in order to inspire and organize his devotees and to preach the Holy Names far and wide.

PRATAPARUDRA WAS THE KING of Orissa at the time, and Sarvabhauma Bhattacharya his court scholar. Sarvabhauma was eager to have Mahaprabhu meet the king, but Mahaprabhu was extremely reluctant to do so. According to the rules of behavior for renunciates, it was forbidden for a sannyasi to meet with any materialistic person, and a king was by definition the most materialistic of all by virtue of his position alone. As a result, Mahaprabhu refused to entertain any such suggestions. When Ramananda Ray retired from his government service and came to live in Puri, the king acted very sympathetically by not only releasing him from his obligations, but awarding him a pension equal to his previous salary as well. Ramananda thus praised Prataparudra to Mahaprabhu, telling him that he was a Vaishnava with all the appropriate qualities.

KING PRATAPARUDRA

Mahaprabhu's heart softened toward the king after hearing Ramananda, but even so, he stuck to his principles.

The seasons changed and Snana Yatra, Lord Jagannath's annual bathing festival, came around. After the bathing festival, the deity of Lord Jagannath is kept out of sight of the public for a fortnight. During this time, Mahaprabhu would go to Alalanath because he could not tolerate being in Puri while Lord Jagannath was indisposed. After the two-week period, he returned to Puri and met with Advaita and other devotees from Bengal who had come to see him and participate in the Rathayatra.

King Prataparudra made sure that all the Bengali Vaishnavas were given proper food and accommodation. Out of their appreciation for the king's service, Nityananda and other devotees asked Mahaprabhu to grant him an audience. When he remained intransigent, Nityananda had to pacify the king by giving him a piece of Mahaprabhu's used cloth. Then, Ramananda arranged for Mahaprabhu to meet the adolescent crown prince, whom Mahaprabhu embraced as a Vaishnava. Mahaprabhu's touch sent the prince into a convulsion of ecstasy, and later, when King Prataparudra touched his son, he too experienced the power of Mahaprabhu's blessings and divine love.

Finally, it was time for the Rathayatra festival. According to the ancient custom, King Prataparudra swept the ground before Lord Jagannath's chariot with a gold-handled broom, and then sprinkled it with sandalwood scented water. Chaitanya

Mahaprabhu observed how the king performed this service in genuine humility and was very pleased by it.

During the pulling of the chariots, Mahaprabhu became absorbed in chanting and dancing as always. When the chariots stopped at the midpoint between the temple and Gundicha, their destination, Mahaprabhu rested in a shaded garden called Balgandi. He was still overcome by the ecstasies of the festival and only half aware of what was going on around him. At this time, King Prataparudra, dressed simply as a Vaishnava, approached Mahaprabhu alone and began to massage his feet. At the same time, he recited the verses from the Srimad Bhagavatam known as "The gopis' song." The following verse was especially dear to Mahaprabhu:

tava kathāmṛtaṁ tapta-jīvanaṁ
kavibhir īḍitaṁ kalmaṣāpaham
śravaṇa-maṅgalaṁ śrīmad-ātataṁ
bhuvi gṛṇanti ye bhūridā janāḥ

> My Lord, your words and the descriptions of your activities are like nectar for those who have been made thirsty in this desert-like material world. Transmitted by exalted personalities, these narrations eradicate all sinful reactions. Whoever hears them attains all good fortune. Those in this world who broadcast these delightful topics are certainly the most munificent altruists.
>
> (*Srimad Bhagavatam* 10.31.9, *Chaitanya Charitamrita* 2.14.14)

As soon as Mahaprabhu heard this verse, he embraced the king. Mahaprabhu recognized him as a genuine humble Vaishnava and no longer saw him as the icon of materialistic culture.

Not long afterward, Mahaprabhu set off on a pilgrimage to Vrindavan. He decided to follow the route along the Ganges, which flows through Bengal. Some legends say that he stopped at Shantipur on this trip and saw his mother for the last time, for Mahaprabhu would never again set foot in the land of his birth. He reached Ramkeli, a village near the capital city, where he met Rupa and Sanatan for the first time. These two brothers were well-known ministers in the government of the ruler, Hussein Shah. Under the influence of Mahaprabhu, Rupa and

NORTH INDIAN PILGRIMAGE

Sanatan soon gave up their ministerial service and accepted the renounced order of life.

Later, when Mahaprabhu was returning from Vrindavan, he met Rupa Goswami in Prayag and then Sanatan in Benares, teaching them both various aspects of devotional philosophy and practice. Mahaprabhu instructed Rupa and Sanatan to go to Vrindavan to recover the lost holy places where Krishna had held his pastimes, to write books on devotional service, and to establish temples where Mahaprabhu in his deity form could be worshiped. These instructions were very significant, because through Rupa and Sanatan, Mahaprabhu established the foundations of the Vaishnava tradition.

LAST YEARS IN JAGANNATH PURI

AFTER TOURING the pilgrimage places in northern India—Vrindavan, Mathura, Prayag, Benares—Mahaprabhu returned to Puri in around 1515, and remained there until his departure from this world in 1533. King Prataparudra's spiritual master Kashi Mishra had a cottage built on his property for Mahaprabhu, known as the Gambhira. Mahaprabhu's interest in external matters diminished day by day. Close devotees like Svarupa Damodar, Ramananda Ray and Paramananda Puri surrounded him. Nevertheless, in the intensity of his absorption in the mood of Srimati Radharani, he became progressively unconscious of the world around him. Extraordinary ecstatic symptoms manifested on Mahaprabhu's body. Sometimes in a state of divine madness, he would run to the entrance of the Jagannath temple and fall down, unconscious.

Sometimes Mahaprabhu would lose himself in the sand dunes on the beach, running toward them with the speed of the wind, taking them to be Govardhan Hill in Vrindavan. Sometimes he would dive into the ocean, thinking it was the Yamuna River, where Krishna had his pastimes. One full moon night, Mahaprabhu was walking with his devotees from one flower garden to another, singing the verses from the Bhagavatam commemorating the Rasa lila. When they came to the garden known as Ai Tota, Mahaprabhu caught a glimpse of the ocean, with the silver effulgence of the moon reflected on its dancing waves. Mahaprabhu's memory of the Yamuna was enkindled and he began to run toward the sea as fast as he was able and jumped into the water. While he was in a trance-like state, seeing himself as a servant of the gopis participating in Krishna's water games in the Yamuna, the outgoing tide pulled his body away from the shore and farther east in the direction of Konark.

None of the other devotees had been able to see where Mahaprabhu had fallen into the water. Svarupa Damodar and the others began to search for him everywhere along the shore. After being unable to find him anywhere, they glumly concluded that he had drowned and would never be seen again. As they were lamenting the loss of Mahaprabhu, Svarupa Damodar saw a fisherman walking on the beach, ecstatically calling out the names of Krishna. Suspecting

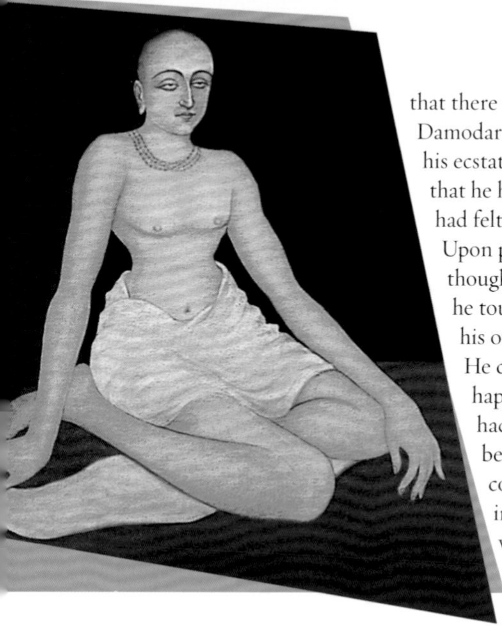

that there was some connection, Svarupa Damodar asked the fisherman the reason for his ecstatic state. The fisherman answered that he had been fishing at night when he had felt something large tugging on his net. Upon pulling it up, he had found what he thought was a dead body, but the moment he touched it, divine ecstasy entered his own body like an electric current. He could not understand what had happened to him and thought that he had caught some kind of supernatural being or ghost. After hearing this account from the fisherman, everyone immediately understood that he was talking about Mahaprabhu and, after reassuring him, insisted on being led to him.

The devotees changed Mahaprabhu into dry clothes. As he returned to a state of semi-awareness, he told them about the visions he had seen: "I went to Vrindavan and saw Krishna there with the gopis, splashing each other and playing hide-and-seek in the waters of the Yamuna. I stood on the shore with the other cowgirls and watched them play."

Every year Chaitanya Mahaprabhu sent someone to Bengal to bring a reassuring message for his mother Sachi, the incarnation of motherly love. One year he sent Jagadananda Pandit, who not only took Mahaprabhu's message, but on Paramananda Puri's request, a piece of Mahaprabhu's cloth and sanctified food from the Jagannath deity. While Jagadananda was in Bengal, he also visited Nabadwip and Shantipur before returning to Puri. This time, Advaita Prabhu gave Mahaprabhu a message in the form of a riddle. The message was:

Mahaprabhu's Pastimes Come to a Close

bāulake kahiha loka ha-ila bāula
bāulake kahiha hāṭe nā bikāya cāula
bāulake kahiha kāje nāhika āula
bāulake kahiha ihā kahiyāche bāula

"Tell that crazy man everyone's gone crazy. Tell that crazy man no one's selling rice in the market. Tell that crazy man there's no more use for crazies like him.

Tell that crazy man that the crazy man said this."
(*Chaitanya Charitamrita* 3.19.20-21)

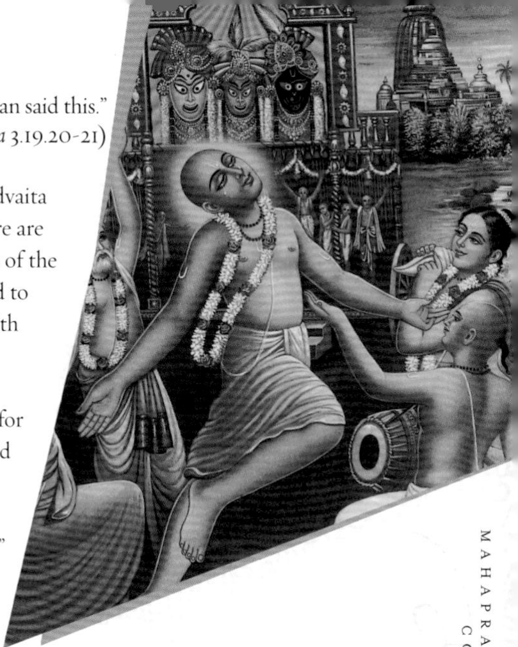

Nobody could understand what Advaita Acharya meant by this riddle. There are still many different interpretations of the verse, but it is generally understood to mean: "Everyone has gone crazy with love for Krishna, so the market for the Holy Name has become saturated. There is thus no more need for Mahaprabhu to remain in the world to spread the religious practice of the age." On hearing the message, Mahaprabhu simply said, "So be it." In other words, he agreed to fulfill Advaita's request. This message signaled the beginning of the last chapter of Mahaprabhu's life in this world. For so long he had been cultivating Radharani's mood, now he lost himself in it completely.

Mahaprabhu's divine madness continued to grow stronger and stronger. One night he rubbed his cheek against the wall of the Gambhira, trying to get out to find Krishna. Svarupa Damodar and Ramananda sang the songs of Chandi Das, Vidyapati and Jayadeva to try to bring him a little peace of mind. On the whole, the last twelve years of Mahaprabhu's life passed in this way. There was barely any difference between his waking and sleeping state.

Most of Mahaprabhu's biographers—Murari Gupta, Kavi Karnapur, Vrindavan Das and Krishna Das Kaviraj—have written nothing about his disappearance. Only Lochan Das writes,

> In the third watch on a Sunday, Mahaprabhu disappeared into Lord Jagannath's body. (*Caitanya-maṅgala*)

According to this account, Mahaprabhu embraced the deity of Lord Jagannath and disappeared into his body in the mid-afternoon one Sunday at the Gundicha temple. Srivasa Pandit, Mukunda Datta, Govinda, Kashi Mishra, and others were present there. They saw Mahaprabhu go into the temple, but when they did not see him come out, they became anxious. They asked the pujari of the Gundicha temple to open the temple doors, but the pujari answered:

> Mahaprabhu has disappeared inside the Gundicha temple. I saw him enter into Jagannath with my own eyes, so I can tell you this with all certainty. (*Caitanya-maṅgala*)

Other people say that Mahaprabhu left his body in the presence of his close friend Gadadhar Pandit, in a state of divine possession, and that his holy remains were buried there on the grounds of the Tota Gopinath temple.

The accounts of Chaitanya Mahaprabhu's life are wondrous indeed, though difficult to fully grasp. The Vedic literatures speak of great saints like Dhruva and avatars like Ramachandra ascending into the spiritual world in the very same body. What then is the reason for doubting that Mahaprabhu could have entered into either Jagannath's body or that of Tota Gopinath?

Chaitanya Mahaprabhu's life is full of many miraculous events and those who find pleasure in hearing about him will be rewarded with spiritual gifts beyond compare.

NAROTTAM DAS THAKUR

NAROTTAM DAS THAKUR lived in the 16th century, in the period immediately following the disappearance of Chaitanya Mahaprabhu. As such, he is considered one of the leaders of the second generation of Gaudiya Vaishnavas. Narottam's name is usually associated with those of Shyamananda Prabhu and Srinivas Acharya, as these three great saints were among the first Bengalis to go to Vrindavan in the post-Chaitanya period in order to study the teachings of the Six Goswamis under Sri Jiva Goswami. On completing their studies, they returned to Bengal, where they popularized these teachings, especially through the medium of song, or kirtan. Narottam Das in particular composed many songs, collected as *Prārthanā* ("Prayers") and *Prema-bhakti-candrikā* ("The Moon Rays of Loving Devotion"), which remain the essential prayer books for all those who follow the Gaudiya Vaishnava tradition.

SWAMI B.B. BODHAYAN is the current president and *acharya* of the Gopinath Gaudiya Math, where he succeeded his own spiritual master, Swami B.P. Puri. He was given the birth name Asim Das on August 21, 1964 in the village of Kanpur, West Bengal. His grandfather, Madan Mohan Das Adhikary, was a direct disciple of Bhaktisiddhanta Saraswati Thakur, who led his entire family to the path of Gaudiya Vaishnavism.

In his childhood, Swami Bodhayan was accustomed to seeing holy men from the Gaudiya Math come regu-

SWAMI B.B. BODHAYAN

larly to his home to visit his grandfather. One of these saintly guests was his eventual spiritual master, Swami B.P. Puri. Every year Swami Bodhayan accompanied his entire family to Sri Mayapur for the annual festivals honoring Srila Prabhupada and Chaitanya Mahaprabhu. These visits to Mayapur instilled in him a deep desire to lead a holy life, though his parents insisted that he first complete his education.

While writing his final high school exams, Swami Bodhayan received the Nrisingha mantra from his guru and began chanting it regularly. He received Harinam initiation in 1986, and was given the *brahmachari* name Achyutananda Das.

Swami Bodhayan joined Swami B.P. Puri's new institution (the Gopinath Gaudiya Math) in 1990, where he took on much of the responsibility for managing its affairs. Over the years he helped open branch maths at Chakra Tirtha in Jagannath Puri and in Vrindavan, as well as publish the organization's monthly journal *Bhāgavata-dharma*, to which he also contributed regularly.

Pleased with the services of his student, Swami B.P. Puri asked him to take sannyas in 1993, on Gaura Purnim. He gave him the new name Tridandi Bhikshu Bhakti Bibudha Bodhayan.

Swami Bodhayan continued to serve his spiritual master, taking on increased responsibility with his new status. Then, on Gaura Purnim, 1997, Puri Maharaj, who was 98 years old, suddenly announced that he was officially making Swami Bodhayan his successor at the helm of the Gopinath Gaudiya Math, designating him president and acharya after his departure. Two years later, when Swami B.P. Puri departed from this world, Swami Bodhayan took over those functions. Since then he has applied himself energetically to teaching the message of Sri Chaitanya Mahaprabhu, following in the footsteps of his spiritual master and Bhaktisiddhanta Saraswati Thakur. His speaking engagements have taken him around the world.

SWAMI B.P. PURI

AGNI DEVA WAS BORN IN TRINIDAD, WEST INDIES, and moved to New York in his youth. His study of Vedic philosophy led him to discover the devotional music of West Bengal. In 1972 he began publicly performing bhajan and kirtan in the traditional Bengali style. He later toured with the South Asian Cultural Exhibition, singing on university campuses throughout the United States. In his numerous trips to India he has sought out master *kirtaniyas* who have helped him evolve a truly traditional style. His influences include the work of A.C.

AGNI DEVA

Bhaktivedanta Swami Prabhupada, from whom he received mantra initiation into the path of pure devotion following Sri Chaitanya. Along with his musical and spiritual pursuits, Agni Deva's other passion is cooking. He owns and operates Govinda's Vegetarian Buffet in Santa Rosa, California.

Kirtan is the sixth recording from Agni Deva, along with *Bhakti Rasa*, *Tribute to Prabhupada*, *Treasure of the Holy Name* and *Live in New Dwarka*. It is the 2nd in the Mandala trilogy, along with *Smaranam* and his upcoming release *Waves of Bhakti*.

A.C. Bhaktivedanta Swami Prabhupada

SONGS & TRANSLATIONS

1

Maha Mantra 1

Hare Krishna Hare Krishna
Krishna Krishna Hare Hare
Hare Rama Hare Rama
Rama Rama Hare Hare

2
Lālasāmayī Prārthanā
WHEN ONE CHANTS THE NAME OF LORD GAURANGA

By Narottam Das Thakur

ONE

'gaurāṅga' bolite habe pulaka-śarīra
'hari hari' bolite nayane ba'be nīra

TWO

āra kabe nitāi-cānder koruṇā hoibe
saṁsāra-bāsanā mora kabe tuccha ha'be

THREE

viṣaya chādiyā kabe śuddha ha'be mon
kabe hāma herabo śrī-bṛndābon

FOUR

rūpa-raghunātha-pade hoibe ākuti
kabe hāma bujhabo se jugala-pīriti

FIVE

rūpa-raghunātha-pade rahu mora āśa
prārthanā koroye sadā narottama-dāsa

ONE

When one chants the name of Gauranga purely, one will experience ecstatic shivering of the body. While chanting the names of Lord Hari, one will have tears in his eyes.

TWO

When I achieve the mercy of Lord Nitai, I will lose all taste for material enjoyment.

THREE

When my mind is completely purified, being freed from material anxieties and desires, then I shall be able to understand Vrindavan.

FOUR

When I am eager to attain the lotus-feet of Srila Rupa Goswami and Srila Raghunath Das Goswami, I will be able to understand the divine pastimes of Sri Sri Radha and Krishna.

FIVE

Always desiring the lotus feet of Rupa and Raghunath, Narottam Das offers this prayer eternally.

3

Aruṇodaya Kīrtan

(part 1)

SUNRISE KIRTAN

By Bhaktivinode Thakur

ONE

udilo aruṇa pūraba-bhāge
dwija-maṇi gorā amani jāge
bhakata-samūha loiyā sāthe
gelā nagara-brāje

TWO

tāthaī tāthaī bājalo khol
ghana ghana tāhe jhāṅjera rol
preme ḍhala ḍhala sonāra aṅga
caraṇe nūpura bāje

THREE

mukunda mādhava jādava hari
bolena bolo re vadana bhori
miche nida-baśe gelo re rāti
divasa śarīra-sāje

FOUR

emana durlabha mānava-deho
pāiyā ki koro bhāvanā keho
ebe nā bhajile jaśodā-suta
carame poribe lāje

FIVE

udita tapana hoile asta
dina gelo boli' hoibe byasta
tabe keno ebe alasa hoi
nā bhaja hṛdoya-rāje

SIX

jīvana anitya jānaha sār
tāhe nānā-vidha vipada-bhār
nāmāśraya kori' jatane tumi
thākaha āpana kāje

SEVEN

jīvera kalyāṇa-sādhana-kām
jagate āsi' e madhura nām
avidyā-timira-tapana-rūpe
hṛd-gagaṇe birāje

EIGHT

kṛṣṇa-nāma-sudhā koriyā pān
jurāo bhakativinoda-prāṇ
nāma binā kichu nāhiko āro
caudda-bhuvana-mājhe

ONE

At the coming of dawn, the jewel among the Brahmins, Lord Gaurasundar woke up and set off with His devotees on a kirtan procession through the town of Nabadwip.

TWO

In the kirtan, mridangas rhythmically resounded täthai täthai while hand cymbals loudly kept the beat. Lord Gauranga's golden form swayed rhythmically in ecstatic love for Krishna and His ankle bells jingled.

THREE

Lord Chaitanya called out to the townsfolk, "You have spent the night in useless sleep and now your day will be spent in taking care of your body! Just call out Krishna's Holy Names with all your heart - Mukunda! Madhava! Yadava! Hari!

FOUR

"You have achieved this rare human body. Do you care nothing for this great gift? If you do not now worship the darling of Mother Yashoda, then a great shame will await you at the time of death.

FIVE

"With every rising and setting of the sun, a day passes and is lost, filling you with anxiety. Why then do you remain idle and not serve the Lord of your heart?

SIX

"You should understand this essential fact: life is temporary and filled with various kinds of miseries. Therefore, carefully take shelter of the Holy Name even while you remain in your occupational duties.

SEVEN

"The sweet name of Krishna has descended into this material universe in order to bless all living entities. It shines like the sun in the sky of the heart, destroying the darkness of ignorance."

EIGHT

Drink the pure nectar of Krishna's Holy Name and thus satisfy the soul of Bhaktivinoda, for there is nothing other than the Holy Name within the fourteen worlds.

Aruṇodaya Kīrtan

(part 2)

WAKE UP! WAKE UP, SLEEPING SOULS!

ONE

jīv jāgo, jīv jāgo, gauracānda bole
kota nidrā jāo māyā-piśācīra kole

TWO

bhajibo boliyā ese saṁsāra-bhitore
bhuliyā rohile tumi avidyāra bhore

THREE

tomāre loite āmi hoinu avatār
āmi binā bandhu āra ke āche tomār

FOUR

enechi auṣadhi māyā nāśibāra lāgi'
hari-nāma mahā-mantra lao tumi māgi'

FIVE

bhakativinoda prabhu-caraṇe pariyā
sei hari-nāma-mantra loilo māgiyā

ONE

Lord Gauranga calls, "Wake up, sleeping souls! Wake up, sleeping souls! You have been sleeping in the lap of the witch Maya far too long!

TWO

"You came into this world promising to worship the Lord, but have forgotten your promise and are lost in the thrall of ignorance.

THREE

"I have descended just to save you. Do you have any friend as kind and helpful to you as I?

FOUR

"I have brought you the medicine that destroys the illusion of Maya, the Maha Mantra. Now take up chanting these names of Krishna with a prayerful attitude."

FIVE

Bhaktivinode falls at the lotus feet of Lord Gauranga and takes up the chanting of the Maha Mantra, begging for mercy.

4

Śrī Nāma Kīrtan

HOLY NAMES TO BE SUNG IN THE STREET

By Bhaktivinode Thakur

ONE

bolo hari bolo (3 times)
manera ānande bhāi bolo hari bolo
bolo hari bolo (3 times)
janame janame sukhe bolo hari bolo

TWO

bolo hari bolo (3 times)
mānaba-janame pe'ye bhāi bolo hari bolo
bolo hari bolo (3 times)
sukhe thāko du˙khe thāko bolo hari bolo

THREE

bolo hari bolo (3 times)
sampade bipade bhāi bolo hari bolo
bolo hari bolo (3 times)
gṛhe thāko bane thāko bolo hari bolo
kṛṣṇera saṁsāre thāki' bolo hari bolo

FOUR

bolo hari bolo (3 times)
asat-saṅga chāḍi' bhāi bolo hari bolo
bolo hari bolo (3 times)
vaiṣṇava-caraṇe paḍi' bolo hari bolo

FIVE

bolo hari bolo (3 times)
gaura-nityānanda bolo (3 times)
gaura-gadādhara bolo (3 times)
gaura-advaita bolo (3 times)

ONE

O my brothers! with joy in your hearts chant, "Hari!" Chant! Chant, "Hari!" Chant! Birth after birth, happily chant, "Hari!" Chant!

TWO

Chant, "Hari!" Chant! O my brothers, now that you have attained this human birth, chant, "Hari!" Chant! Chant, "Hari!" Chant! In happiness or in suffering, chant, "Hari!" Chant!

THREE

Chant, "Hari!" Chant! O my brothers, in good times or in bad, chant, "Hari!" Chant! Chant, "Hari!" Chant! Stay at home, or stay in the forest, but chant, "Hari!" Chant! As long as you stay in this world that belongs to Lord Krishna, chant, "Hari!" Chant!

FOUR

Chant, "Hari!" Chant! Shun the wicked, O my brothers, and chant, "Hari!" Chant! Chant, "Hari!" Chant! Bow down before a true Vaishnava's feet and chant, "Hari!" Chant!

FIVE

Chant, "Hari!" Chant! Chant, "Gaura-Nityananda!" Chant, "Gaura-Gadadhara!" Chant, "Gaura-Advaita!" Chant!

5

Śrī Nagara-saṅkīrtan

STREET SANKIRTAN

By Bhaktivinode Thakur

ONE

nadīyā godrume nityānanda mahājan
patiyāche nām-haṭṭa jīvera kāraṇ

TWO

(śraddhāvān jan he! śraddhāvān jan he!)
prabhura ājñāy bhāi, māgi ei bhikhā
bolo kṛṣṇa, bhajo kṛṣṇa, koro kṛṣṇa śīkhā

THREE

aparādha-śūnya ho'ye, loho kṛṣṇa nām
kṛṣṇa mātā, kṛṣṇa pitā, kṛṣṇa dhana-prāṇ

FOUR

kṛṣṇera saṁsāra koro, chāri'anācār
jīve doyā kṛṣṇa-nām sarva-dharma sār

ONE

On the island of Godruma in Nabadwip Dham, the magnanimous Lord Nityananda has opened up the Marketplace of the Holy Name, meant for the deliverance of all fallen souls.

TWO

O men of faith! O men of faith! On Lord Gauranga's order, brothers, I beg this one thing of you: Chant Krishna's name, worship Krishna, and learn about Krishna.

THREE

Being careful to remain free of offenses, just repeat the Holy Name of Krishna. Krishna is your mother, Krishna is your father, and Krishna is the treasure of your very life.

FOUR

Giving up all improper behavior, carry on your worldly duties only in relation to Krishna. Chanting the Holy Name of Krishna and showing compassion to all living beings is the essence of all religion.

6
Dayā Koro More
PRAYER FOR MERCY

By Narottam Das Thakur

ONE

śrī kṛṣṇa caitanya prabhu dayā koro more
tomā vinā ke dayālu jagat saṁsāre

TWO

patita pāvana hetu tava avatār
mo-sama patita prabhu nā pāibe ār

THREE

hā hā prabhu nityānanda premānanda sukhī
kṛpāvalokana koro āmi boro duḥkhī

FOUR

dayā koro sītā-pati advaita gosāñi
tava kṛpā-bale pāi caitanya-nitāi

FIVE

hā hā svarūpa sanātana rūpa raghunāth
bhaṭṭa-juga śrī-jīva hā prabhu lokanāth

SIX

dayā koro śrī-ācārya prabhu śrīnivās
rāmacandra saṅga māge narottama dās

ONE

O Lord Krishna Chaitanya, please be merciful to me. Who in this world is more compassionate than you?

TWO

You have descended into this world in order to deliver the most fallen souls. You will not find a soul anywhere who is more fallen than I.

THREE

O Nityananda! You are immersed in the joy of divine love. Please look kindly on me, for I am completely miserable.

FOUR

O Advaita Prabhu, husband of Sita Devi! By the power of your grace I hope to attain the service of Lord Chaitanya and Lord Nityananda.

FIVE

O Svarupa Damodar! O Sanatan Goswami! O Rupa Goswami! O Raghunath! O Gopal Bhatta! O Raghunath Bhatta! O my spiritual master, Lokanath Prabhu!

SIX

O Srinivas Acharya! Please be merciful to me and grant me the association of Ramachandra Kaviraj. Thus prays Narottam Das.

7

Nāma-saṅkīrtan 1

SINGING THE NAMES OF THE LORD

By Narottam Das Thakur

ONE

hari haraye nama˙ kṛṣṇa yādavāya namaha˙
yādavāya mādhavāya keśavāya namaha˙

TWO

gopāla govinda rāma śrī-madhusūdan
giridhārī gopīnātha madana-mohan

THREE

śrī-caitanya-nityānanda śrī-advaita-sītā
hari guru vaiṣṇava bhāgavata gītā

FOUR

śrī-rūpa sanātana bhaṭṭa-raghunāth
śrī-jīva gopāla-bhaṭṭa dāsa-raghunāth

FIVE

ei chay gosāir kori caraṇa vandan
jāhā hoite bighna-nāś abhīṣṭa-pūraṇ

SIX

ei chay gosāi jār—mui tār dās
tā-sabāra pada-reṇu mora pañca-grās

SEVEN

tādera caraṇa-sebi-bhakta-sane bās
janame janame hoy ei abhilāṣ

EIGHT

ei chay gosāi jabe braje koilā bās
rādhā-kṛṣṇa-nitya-līlā korilā prakāś

NINE

ānande bolo hari bhaja vṛndāvan
śrī-guru-vaiṣṇava-pade majāiyā man

TEN

śrī-guru-vaiṣṇava-pāda-padma kori āś
nāma-saṅkīrtana kohe narottama dās

ONE

O Lord Hari, O Lord Krishna, I offer my obeisances to You, who are known as Yadava, Hari, Madhava, and Keshava.

TWO

O Gopal, Govinda, Rama, Sri Madhusudana, Giridhari, Gopinath, Madan Mohan!

THREE

All glories to Sri Chaitanya and Nityananda. All glories to Sri Advaita Acharya and His consort, Sri Sita Thakurani. All glories to Lord Hari, the spiritual master, the Vaishnavas, Srimad Bhagavatam, and Srimad Bhagavad Gita.

FOUR

All glories to Sri Rupa Goswami, Sanatan Goswami, Raghunath Bhatta Goswami, Sri Jiva Goswami, Gopal Bhatta Goswami, and Raghunath Das Goswami.

FIVE

I offer my obeisances to the feet of these six Goswamis. By offering them obeisances, all obstacles to devotion are destroyed and all spiritual desires are fulfilled.

SIX

I am the servant of anyone who serves these six Goswamis. The dust of their holy feet is my five kinds of foodstuffs.

SEVEN

This is my desire, that birth after birth I may live with those devotees who serve the lotus feet of the six Goswamis.

EIGHT

When the six Goswamis lived in Vraja they revealed and explained the eternal pastimes of Radha and Krishna.

NINE

Absorbing your mind in meditation upon the divine feet of the spiritual master and the holy Vaishnavas, chant the names of Lord Hari in ecstasy and worship the transcendental realm of Vrindavan.

TEN

Desiring the lotus feet of Sri Guru and the Vaishnavas, Narottam Das sings this litany of Holy Names.

8

Gaurāṅgera Duṭi Pada

LORD GAURANGA'S LOTUS FEET

By Narottam Das Thakur

ONE

gaurāṅgera duṭi pada, jār dhana sampada
se jāne bhakati-rasa-sār
gaurāṅgera madhura-līlā, jār karṇe prabeśilā
hṛdoya nirmala bhelo tār

TWO

je gaurāṅgera nāma loy, tāra hoy premodoy
tāre mui jāi bolihāri
gaurāṅga-guṇete jhure, nitya-līlā tāre sphure
se jana bhakati-adhikārī

THREE

gaurāṅgera saṅgi-gaṇe, nitya-siddha kori māne
se jāy brajendra-suta-pāś
śrī-gauḍa-maṇḍala-bhūmi, jeba jāne cintāmaṇi
tāra hoy braja-bhūme bās

FOUR

gaura-prema-rasārṇave, se taraṅge jebā ḍube
se rādhā-mādhava-antaraṅga
gṛhe bā banete thāke, hā gaurāṅga bole ḍāke
narottama māge tāra saṅga

ONE

Anyone who has accepted Lord Gauranga's lotus feet can understand the true essence of devotional service. If one is captivated by the pleasing pastimes of Lord Chaitanya, the dirty things in his heart will all be cleansed.

TWO

Anyone who chants the name of Lord Gauranga, will immediately develop love of God. To such a person I offer all congratulations. If one appreciates the merciful pastimes of Lord Chaitanya and feels ecstasy and sometimes cries, this process will immediately help him to understand the eternal pastimes of Radha-Krishna.

THREE

Simply by understanding that Lord Gauranga's associates are eternally free from material contamination, one can immediately be promoted to the transcendental abode of Lord Krishna. If one simply understands that the land of Nabadwip is not different from Vrindavan, then he actually lives in Vrindavan.

FOUR

If one says: "Let me dive deep into the waves of the nectarean ocean of the transcendental loving movement introduced by Lord Chaitanya," he immediately becomes one of the confidential devotees of Radha and Krishna. It does not matter whether one is a householder living at home or a vanaprastha or sannyasi living in the forest, if he chants "O Gauranga!" and becomes a devotee of Lord Chaitanya, then Narottam Das begs to have his association.

9
Maha Mantra 2

Hare Krishna Hare Krishna
Krishna Krishna Hare Hare
Hare Rama Hare Rama
Rama Rama Hare Hare

THE HARMONIUM - The harmonium is a western instrument that originated in Germany and England and became popular among immigrant pioneers in the American West in the 19th century. Around the same time, the British brought the harmonium to India, where it was quickly absorbed into the Indian music culture. Though not a traditional Indian instrument, it was admired for its portability and drone quality, which made it uniquely appropriate to the Indian aesthetic.

THE CELLO - The cello was first made in its current shape in the mid 1600's. Its predecessor was the viola da gamba (Italian for knee fiddle), which had 6 or 7 strings and tied frets across its finger board. The current design of the cello allows the artist to play with a more melodic and expressive approach (instead of the viola da gamba's chordal approach), a development consistent with the changes of European music during the seventeenth century.

INSTRUMENTS

MRIDANGA - The word mridanga is derived from mrid "clay" and anga "body," meaning that it is an instrument, a drum in this case, whose body or shell is made of clay. According to other sources, it derives from mridan and ga, meaning "beaten while moving," as its design permits the drum to be hung around the neck and played while walking or even dancing.

This instrument has a unique history connected to the cultural and spiritual revolution of Sri Chaitanya in sixteenth century Bengal. It is said that Sri Chaitanya ordered his associates to construct clay drums instead of the heavy and costly wooden drums.

A number of styles of mridanga playing developed known as Manoharshayi, Mandarini and Garanhati. These schools trace their lineages back to Srinivas Acharya, Shyamananda Pandit, and Narottam Das Thakur respectively. Though these ancient traditions have undergone change and are little practiced in their original form, the mridanga continues to be popular in Vaishnava sacred music.

According to the Manoharshayi school, Lord Krishna's flute pleaded with him not to be left behind when he became incarnate as Sri Chaitanya. Krishna thus allowed the flute to accompany him in his advent as Sri Chaitanya in the mridanga form.

It is also said that Sri Chaitanya prayed to Lord Jagannath for the mantras with which to play the mridanga and the revelation of these mantras was given to Gadadhar Pandit who became the first player of this divine instrument.

HARMONIUM

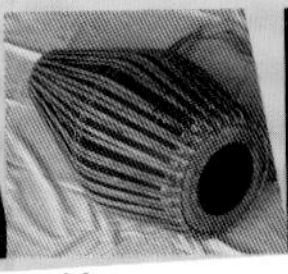
MRIDANGA

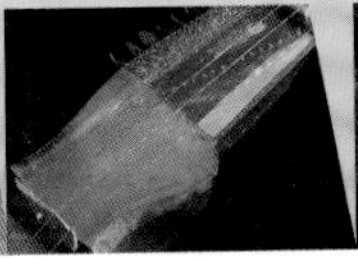
SARANGI

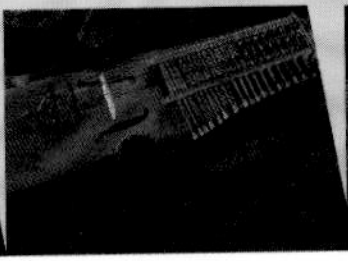
NYCKELHARPA

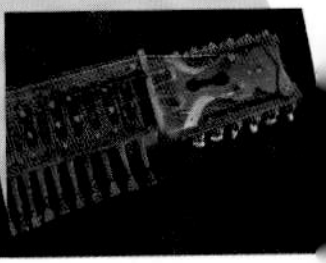
SITARA

namo jagannātha-sutāya
namo mṛdaṅga lavanāṅga-rasa-mādhurī
sahasra-guṇa-saṁyuktaṁ
namo mṛdaṅga namo namaḥ
namo baladevāya namo namaḥ

SARANGI - The sarangi is a bowed Indian fiddle with a goatskin top that is played with the cuticles of the left hand. It has three main strings and 36 resonating strings that are grouped into four different tuned sets. Unlike the sitar or sarod, which were played at the courts of medieval Indian nobility, the sarangi is considered to be a folklore instrument that was primarily used to accompany singers. Its popularity declined as the aforementioned instruments gained more and more recognition. The instrument used on this recording was built by Ricki Ram in Delhi and modified by Hans Christian.

NYCKELHARPA - The nyckelharpa is a bowed Scandinavian key fiddle, with four main strings and 12 resonating strings. The player pushes a set of wooden keys which in turn press against the strings. It's origins extend back to the Middle Ages.

SITARA - The sitara is a mini version of the Indian sitar with curved brass frets, four play strings, eight resonating strings, and two arched bridges that create the characteristic buzzing sound. The particular instrument played by Hans is custom made from solid ebony by a San Francisco Bay Area instrument maker.

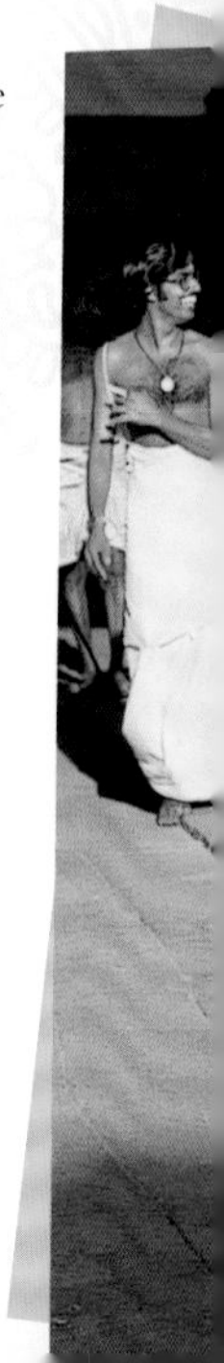

1. *Maha Mantra 1*

Agni Deva- *lead vocals, kartals*
Markandeya- *tablas*
Vinode Vani- *harmonium*
Hans Christian- *sarangi, cello, bass, keyboards*
Choir- *response vocals*

2. *Lālasāmayī Prārthanā*

Agni Deva- *lead vocals, kartals*
Bhima Karma- *mridanga*
Vinode Vani- *harmonium*
Hans Christian- *cello, bass, shakers, keyboards*
Choir- *response vocals*

3. *Aruṇodaya Kīrtan*

Agni Deva- *lead vocals, kartals*
Bhima Karma- *mridanga*
Vinode Vani- *harmonium*
Hans Christian- *sarangi, cello, bass, keyboards, add. harmonium*
Kim Waters- *shakers*
Choir- *response vocals*

4. *Śrī Nāma Kīrtan*

Agni Deva- *lead vocals, kartals*
Bhima Karma- mridanga
Vinode Vani- *harmonium*
Hans Christian- *bass, shakers, keyboards*
Kim Waters- *bells*
Choir- *response vocals*

5. *Śrī Nagara-saṅkīrtan*

Agni Deva- *lead vocals, kartals*
Bhima Karma- *mridanga*
Vinode Vani- *harmonium*
Hans Christian- *cello, bass, shakers, percussion, keyboards, tambura*
Choir- *response vocals*

6. *Dayā Koro More*

Agni Deva- *lead vocals, kartals*
Markandeya- *mridanga*
Vinode Vani- *harmonium*
Hans Christian- *sarangi, sitara, cello, bass, percussion, keyboards,*
Choir- *response vocals*

7. *Nāma-saṅkīrtan*

Agni Deva- *lead vocals, kartals*
Bhima Karma- *mridanga*
Vinode Vani- *harmonium*
Hans Christian- *bass, shakers, keyboards*
Choir- *response vocals*

8. *Gaurāṅgera duṭi pada*

Agni Deva- *lead vocals, kartals*
Markandeya- *mridanga*
Vinode Vani- *harmonium*
Hans Christian- *sitara, cello, bass*
Choir- *response vocals*

9. *Maha Mantra 2*

Agni Deva- *lead vocals, kartals*
Bhima Karma- *mridanga*
Vinode Vani- *harmonium*
Hans Christian- *sarangi, cello, bass, percussion, keyboards, additional harmonium*
Choir- *response vocals*

Kirtan Choir: Nidra N. Kilmer, Manjari Ehrlichman, Prema Mayi Groover, Navadwipa Das, Ramdas Das and Syamasundar Das.

Produced by Hans Christian and Mandala Media - Executive Producer- Raoul Goff. Recorded, mixed and mastered at Allemande Music, Sister Bay, WI

SONG credits

TRACK *list*

Mandala Publishing
17 Paul Drive
San Rafael, CA 94903
www.mandala.org
800.688.2218

Library of Congress Cataloging-in-Publication Data available.

ISBN10: 1-932771-95-6
ISBN13: 978-1-932771-95-4

PALACE PRESS INTERNATIONAL

americanforests.org GLOBAL RELEAF

REPLANTED PAPER

Palace Press International, in association with
Global ReLeaf, will plant two trees for each tree used
in the manufacturing of this book. Global ReLeaf is an
international campaign by American Forests, the nation's
oldest nonprofit conservation organization and a world
leader in planting trees for environmental restoration.

10 9 8 7 6 5 4 3 2 1